OLYMPIC
RECORDS

BY THOMAS K. ADAMSON

BLASTOFF!
DISCOVERY

Bellwether Media • Minneapolis, MN

Blastoff! Discovery launches a new mission: reading to learn. Filled with facts and features, each book offers you an exciting new world to explore!

This edition first published in 2018 by Bellwether Media, Inc.

No part of this publication may be reproduced in whole or in part without written permission of the publisher.
For information regarding permission, write to Bellwether Media, Inc., Attention: Permissions Department,
5357 Penn Avenue South, Minneapolis, MN 55419.

Library of Congress Cataloging-in-Publication Data

Names: Adamson, Thomas K., 1970- author.
Title: Olympic Records / by Thomas K. Adamson.
Description: Minneapolis, MN : Bellwether Media, Inc., 2018.
   | Series: Blastoff! Discovery. Incredible Sports Records |
   Includes bibliographical references and index.
Identifiers: LCCN 2017032285 (print) |
   LCCN 2017032986 (ebook) | ISBN 9781626177857
   (hardcover : alk. paper) | ISBN 9781618913159
   (pbk. : alk. paper) | ISBN 9781681034966 (ebook)
Subjects: LCSH: Olympics–Records–Juvenile literature.
Classification: LCC GV721.8 (ebook) | LCC GV721.8 .A34
   20148 (print) | DDC 796.48068–dc23
LC record available at https://lccn.loc.gov/2017032285

Editor: Nathan Sommer   Designer: Steve Porter

Printed in the United States of America, North Mankato, MN.

TABLE OF CONTENTS

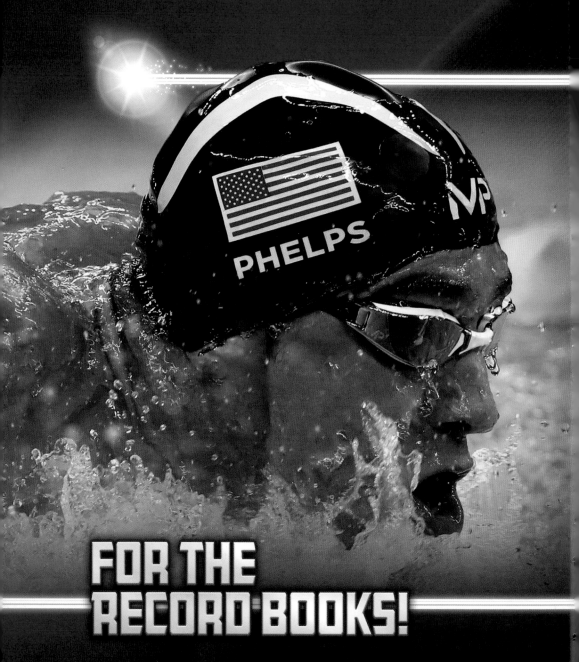

FOR THE RECORD BOOKS!

Winning a gold medal is any Olympian's dream. Standing atop the **podium** is a major accomplishment. Many have been repeat Olympic champions. But no one has matched American swimmer Michael Phelps.

Phelps won gold in eight different events during the 2008 Games. He broke world records in all but one. His record eight golds at one Games will be hard to beat. Unbelievable Olympic displays like Phelps' amaze the world. Read on to learn about other incredible Olympic records!

RECORD-BREAKING CHAMPIONS

Olympic champions are the best at what they do. They compete in front of hundreds of millions of people. Some win big. Others rise above the rest to become icons forever.

Olympic **100-meter dash** winners earn the nickname "world's fastest human." Jamaica's Usain Bolt claimed this title a record three straight times. Bolt sped past everyone else from 2008 to 2016. This makes him one of the best Olympic sprinters ever!

BOLT OF LIGHTNING

Bolt's 100-meter dash time of 9.63 seconds in 2012 is also an Olympic record.

MOST CONSECUTIVE 100-METER DASH GOLD MEDALS

Record: **3 gold medals**

Record holder: **Usain Bolt**

Year record was set: **2016**

Former record holder: **Carl Lewis**

How long previous record stood: **28 years**

American Bob Beamon holds
an unforgettable Olympic record.
His **long jump** at the 1968
games was 1.8 feet (0.5 meters)
farther than the past record.
The judge's tools were too short
to measure Beamon's landing.
They had to use a tape measure
to figure it out!

FARTHEST
MEN'S LONG JUMP

Record: 8.9 meters (29.2 feet)
Record holder: Bob Beamon
Year record was set: 1968
Former record holder: Ralph Boston
How long previous record stood:
8 years

Germany's Birgit Fischer was a top Olympic **kayaker** for many years. She won 12 medals in the sport, including eight golds. Fischer dominated in both individual and team events. She is the only female Olympian to win gold at six different Games!

YOUNGEST AND OLDEST CHAMPION

Birgit Fischer is the youngest and oldest gold medalist in kayaking. She won her first gold at age 18 and her last at 42.

MOST OLYMPIC GAMES WITH A GOLD MEDAL, FEMALE

Record: 6 Olympic Games
Record holder: Birgit Fischer
Year record was set: 2004
Former record holder:
broke her own record
How long previous record stood:
4 years

Norway's Ole Einar Bjørndalen is the most accomplished Winter Olympian. He has won 13 medals in **biathlon**. This unusual sport mixes **cross-country skiing** and **target shooting**. In 2002, he won gold in every event he competed in!

Gymnast Larisa Latynina held the record for most medals before Phelps. She won 18 medals for the Soviet Union.

MOST OLYMPIC MEDALS, ALL-TIME

Record: 28 medals

Record holder: Michael Phelps

Year record was set: 2016

Former record holder:

broke his own record

How long previous record stood: 4 years

In 2016, Michael Phelps became the Olympics' most winning champion. He won his 28th medal at his fourth Olympic Games that year. Phelps took home 2 bronze, 3 silver, and an amazing 23 gold medals over the years.

RECORD-BREAKING TEAMS

Team athletes depend on each other to find success. They must compete well together. When they are good at this, the sky is the limit in terms of what they can accomplish.

The United States has the most gold medals in basketball. Many of these are thanks to its dominating women's team. It holds the record for most **consecutive** gold medals. The team has won six straight golds through the 2016 games!

THE CENTURY MARK

In 2016, the U.S. women's basketball team also became the first to score over 100 points in three straight games.

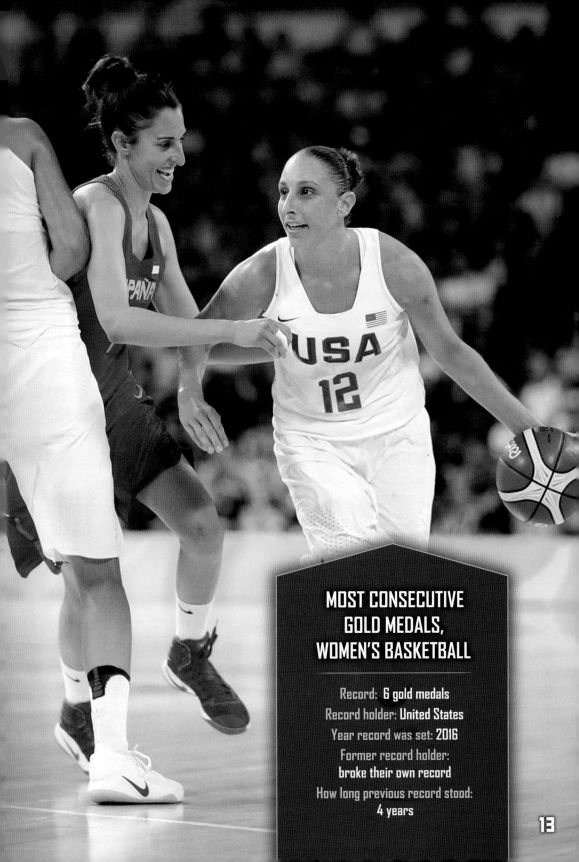

MOST CONSECUTIVE GOLD MEDALS, WOMEN'S BASKETBALL

Record: 6 gold medals
Record holder: United States
Year record was set: 2016
Former record holder:
broke their own record
How long previous record stood:
4 years

13

Beach volleyball became an Olympic sport in 1996. No team has been better than Misty May-Treanor and Kerri Walsh Jennings since then. They won three gold medals from 2004 to 2012. Millions tuned in to watch them win 21 straight **matches**.

MOST GOLD MEDALS, BEACH VOLLEYBALL

Record: 3 gold medals
Record holders: Misty May-Treanor and Kerri Walsh Jennings
Year record was set: 2012
Former record holders:
broke their own record
How long previous record stood:
4 years

The 2016 U.S. women's gymnastics team called themselves "The Final Five." Their great coach, Marta Károlyi, retired after the Games that year.

LARGEST MARGIN OF VICTORY, TEAM GYMNASTICS

Record: 8.209 points
Record holder: U.S. women's gymnastics team
Year record was set: 2016
Former record holder: broke their own record
How long previous record stood: 4 years

The U.S. women's gymnastics team was favored to win gold at the 2016 Games. But no one thought they would win by so much! They finished 8.209 points ahead of Russia. It was the largest victory ever under the current scoring system.

Sisters Venus and Serena Williams ruled Olympic women's tennis for years. Their three gold medals in **doubles** competition is an Olympic record. The Williams sisters are also great players on their own. Each has won a gold medal in **singles** competition!

MOST GOLD MEDALS, DOUBLES TENNIS

Record: 3 gold medals
Record holders: Venus and Serena Williams
Year record was set: 2012
Former record holders:
Gigi Fernández and Mary Joe Fernández
How long previous record stood: 16 years

BEST TIME IN MEN'S ROWING, COXLESS PAIR

Record: 6:08.5
Record holders: Hamish Bond and Eric Murray
Year record was set: 2012
Former record holders: Steven Redgrave and Matthew Pinsent
How long previous record stood: 16 years

Rowers Hamish Bond and Eric Murray knew how to win. This New Zealand team broke the world record for best time in the **coxless pair** event in 2012. Their time of 6:08.5 beat the old record by almost 12 seconds!

RECORD-BREAKING SCORES

Many Olympic events score athletes on their performance. Athletes work very hard to reach perfection. But only few get that perfect score.

Romanian gymnast Nadia Comăneci scored the first perfect 10 in Olympic history in 1976. Comăneci wowed judges with her display in the **uneven bars** event. The 14-year-old did not stop there. She ended up earning seven perfect 10s that year!

OUTSMARTING THE SCOREBOARD

The judges' scoreboards were unable to display the score of 10 at the time. Comăneci's perfect 10s were shown as "1.0."

MOST PERFECT 10s, GYMNASTICS

Record: **7 perfect 10 scores**
Record holder: **Nadia Comăneci**
Year record was set: 1976
Former record holder: N/A
How long previous record stood: N/A

American snowboarder Shaun White is a master of the **half-pipe**. He won back-to-back golds in 2006 and 2010. White scored 48.4 out of 50 during his second ride in 2010. It was the highest Olympic half-pipe score ever!

BEST SCORE, SNOWBOARD HALF-PIPE

Record: 48.4

Record holder: **Shaun White**

Year record was set: 2010

Former record holder: broke his own record

How long previous record stood: 4 years

They say nobody is perfect. But the Canadian women's **curling** team was at the 2014 Winter Games. The team won every match on their way to gold that year. They are the only women's curling team to go undefeated at the Olympics!

BEST RECORD IN ONE GAMES, WOMEN'S CURLING

Record: undefeated Olympic run
Record holder: Canada
Year record was set: 2014
Former record holder: N/A
How long previous record stood: N/A

Some Olympic scores are more about strength than style. Lasha Talakhadze from the country of Georgia holds the record for weightlifting in the **super heavyweight** class. He lifted a combined 1,043 pounds (473 kilograms) during the 2016 Summer Games!

MOST COMBINED WEIGHT LIFTED, SUPER HEAVYWEIGHT CLASS

Record: 1,043 pounds (473 kilograms)
Record holder: Lasha Talakhadze
Year record was set: 2016
Former record holder:
Hossein Rezazadeh
How long previous record stood:
16 years

Mitcham was the first Australian diver to win gold in 84 years.

HIGHEST SCORE FOR A SINGLE DIVE, 10-METER PLATFORM DIVING

Record: 112.10 points
Record holder: Matthew Mitcham
Year record was set: 2008
Former record holder:
broke his own record
How long previous record stood:
one day

Australian diver Matthew Mitcham needed a great dive to win gold in 2008. He definitely delivered! Mitcham's final dive in the **10-meter platform** event that year was nearly perfect. His 112.10-point score earned him a gold medal and an Olympic record!

RECORD-BREAKING TIMES

Olympic races are timed carefully. Half of a second could be the difference between winning gold and missing the podium entirely. Some times are greater than what seems possible!

Jamaica has proven to have the best sprinters at multiple Olympics. In 2012, the team of Carter, Frater, Blake, and Bolt finished the 4x100-meter **relay** with a record time of 36.84 seconds. No team had ever finished the race in under 37 seconds before!

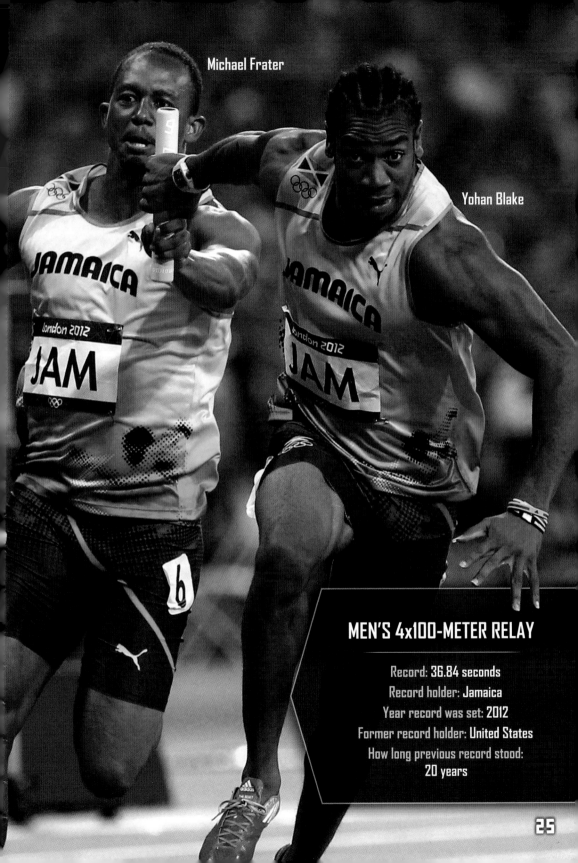

Michael Frater

Yohan Blake

MEN'S 4x100-METER RELAY

Record: 36.84 seconds
Record holder: Jamaica
Year record was set: 2012
Former record holder: United States
How long previous record stood:
20 years

Ethiopia's Kenenisa Bekele narrowly missed winning gold in the 2004 5,000-meter run. He returned with something to prove in 2008. Bekele led the race from the start this time. His record-breaking time of 12:57.82 earned him gold!

CLEAN SWEEP

Bekele also broke the Olympic record in the 10,000-meter race in 2008.

MEN'S 5,000-METER RUN

Record: 12:57.82
Record holder: Kenenisa Bekele
Year record was set: 2008
Former record holder: Saïd Aouita
How long previous record stood:
24 years

Ω OMEGA

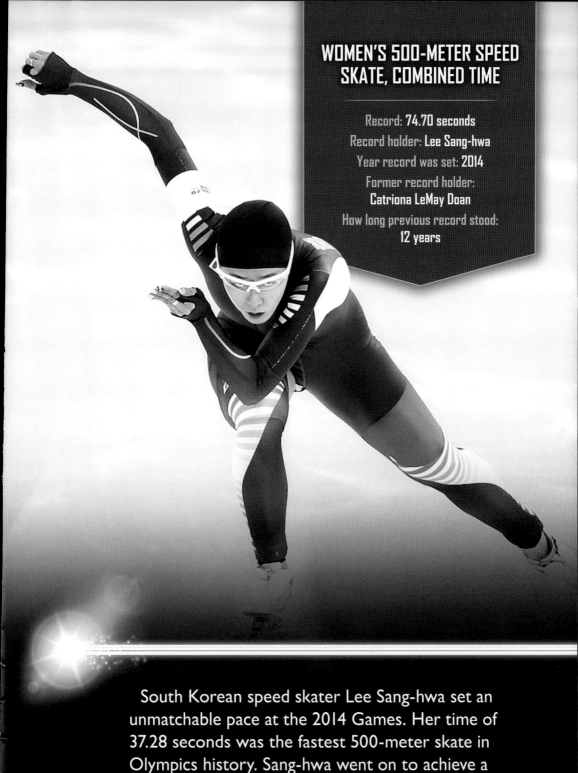

Record: 74.70 seconds
Record holder: Lee Sang-hwa
Year record was set: 2014
Former record holder:
Catriona LeMay Doan
How long previous record stood:
12 years

South Korean speed skater Lee Sang-hwa set an unmatchable pace at the 2014 Games. Her time of 37.28 seconds was the fastest 500-meter skate in Olympics history. Sang-hwa went on to achieve a record-shattering combined time of 74.70 seconds for two races that year!

Florence Griffith Joyner gave the best display of female sprinting ever in 1988. She smashed the records in the 100-meter and 200-meter dashes that year. Her outstanding 200-meter dash time of 21.34 seconds also broke the world record!

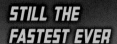

STILL THE FASTEST EVER

Griffith Joyner still holds the world and Olympic records in the 100-meter and 200-meter races.

WOMEN'S 200-METER DASH

Record: 21.34 seconds
Record holder: Florence Griffith Joyner
Year record was set: 1988
Former record holder:
Valerie Brisco-Hooks
How long previous record stood:
4 years

800-METER FREESTYLE

Record: 8:04.79
Record holder: Katie Ledecky
Year record was set: 2016
Former record holder: Rebecca Adlington
How long previous record stood: 8 years

American Katie Ledecky was the best female swimmer at the 2016 Games. She finished more than 11 seconds ahead of the next best swimmer during the 800-meter **freestyle** race. Her 8:04.79 time was an Olympic and world record. She truly is an Olympic champion!

GLOSSARY

10-meter platform—a diving event in which the diver jumps off a solid platform 10 meters (32.8 feet) above the water

100-meter dash—a sprinting race that covers a distance of 100 meters (328 feet)

biathlon—a winter event that combines cross-country skiing and rifle target shooting

consecutive—one right after the other

coxless pair—a rowing event in which two athletes move a boat using oars

cross-country skiing—a form of skiing in which skiers use their own power to move over long distances

curling—a winter sport in which two teams slide stones over ice toward a target

doubles—a tennis competition with a two-player team on each side of the court

freestyle—a swimming race in which swimmers may use any swimming stroke

half-pipe—a snowboarding event that takes place in a large U-shaped ramp that looks like half of a pipe

kayaker—an athlete who paddles a kayak; a kayak is a small, narrow boat with an opening in the top for people to sit.

long jump—an event in which a jump for distance is made from a running start

matches—the series of games in volleyball that determine the winner; the winner must win two out of three games in the match.

podium—a raised platform

relay—a team race in which each athlete covers part of the total distance

rowers—athletes who row a boat in races; rowers row their boat with oars as individuals or in crews of two, four, or eight.

singles—a tennis competition with one player on each side of the court

super heavyweight—a weightlifting class for athletes who weigh more than 231 pounds (105 kilograms) for men and 165 pounds (75 kilograms) for women

target shooting—a competition involving firing a gun at a target; higher scores are awarded to the most accurate shots.

uneven bars—a gymnastics event with two bars that are set at different heights above the floor

TO LEARN MORE

AT THE LIBRARY

Radnedge, Keir. *Olympic and World Records*. London: Carlton Books, 2016.

Rosen, Karen. *Great Moments in Olympic Track & Field*. Minneapolis, Minn.: Abdo Publishing, 2015.

Westcott, Jim. *Olympic Greats*. Mankato, Minn.: Black Rabbit Books, 2018.

ON THE WEB

Learning more about Olympic records
is as easy as 1, 2, 3.

1. Go to www.factsurfer.com.

2. Enter "Olympic records" into the search box.

3. Click the "Surf" button and you will see a list of related web sites.

With factsurfer.com, finding more information is just a click away.

INDEX

The images in this book are reproduced through the courtesy of: FRANCOIS-XAVIER MARIT/ Getty Images, front cover; janniwet, front cover (gold around text), p. 3 (gold around text); cobalt88, pp. 2-32 (flashes); Waj, pp. 2-3 (silver background), 30-31 (silver background), 32 (silver background); mezzotint, pp. 2-3 (runner); Clive Rose/ Getty Images, p. 4; PCN Black/ Alamy, p. 5; dpa picture alliance/ Alamy, pp. 6-7; Ed Lacey/ Popperfoto/ Getty Images, p. 8; MLADEN ANTONOV/ Getty Images, p. 9; Agence Zoom/ Getty Images, p. 10; Al Bello/ Getty Images, p. 11; Tim Clayton - Corbis/ Getty Images, pp. 12-13; Charlotte Observer/ Getty Images, p. 14; BEN STANSALL/ Getty Images, p. 15; Mark Humphrey/ AP Images, p. 16; Phil Walter/ Getty Images, p. 17; Sport The Library/ Newscom, pp. 18-19; Tara Walton/ AP Images, p. 20; JUNG YEON-JE/ Getty Images, p. 21; Paul Kitagaki Jr./ Alamy, p. 22; Adam Pretty/ Getty Images, p. 23; Kyodo/ AP Images, p. 24; Cameron Spencer/ Getty Images, pp. 24-25; Allstar Picture Library/ Alamy, p. 26; Quinn Rooney/ Getty Images, p. 27; Tony Duffy/ Getty Images, p. 28; Harry How, p. 29.